Not Your M...

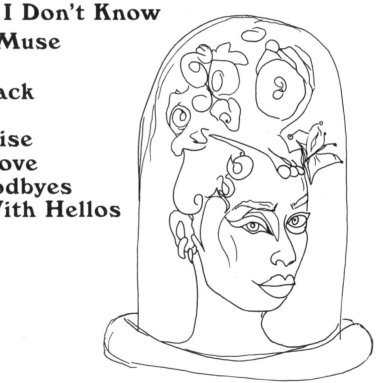

Written & Performed by
Celeste

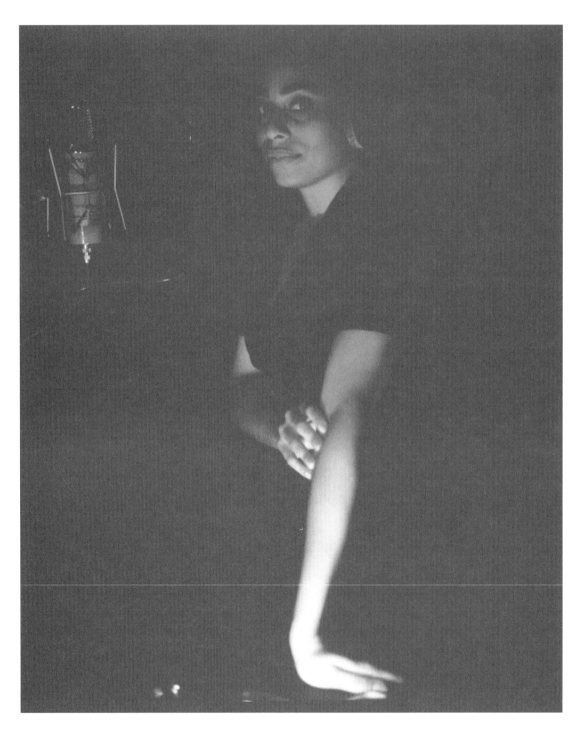

Me recording 'Ideal Woman' - September 2020

Photograph by Jesse Crankson

Ideal Woman

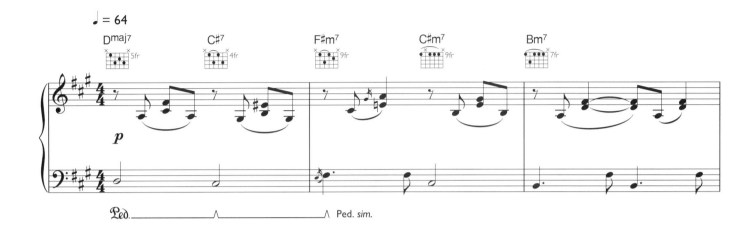

1. I___ like to think   it's be-cause   I'm___ too proud,_____   too proud,   too proud, too

(2.) look good,_____   too good,   too good, too

___ loud.___

___ good.___

Some oth-ers may say it's___ be-cause   I'm___ so tall,_____

Some oth-ers may say it's___ be-cause I lack pa-tience, always

Words and Music by Celeste Waite and Josh Crocker

Dominic Canning – broken finger but still going!

Strange

Words and Music by Celeste Waite, Jamie Hartman, Stephen Wrabel and Eric Leva

2. Back to this room,_____ back to our roots,_____

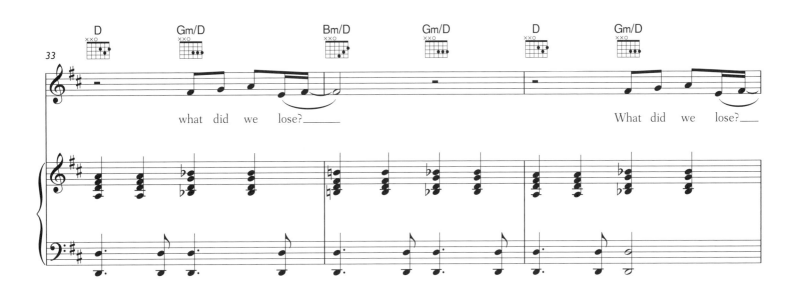

what did we lose?_____ What did we lose?____

D.%. al Coda   ⊕ Coda

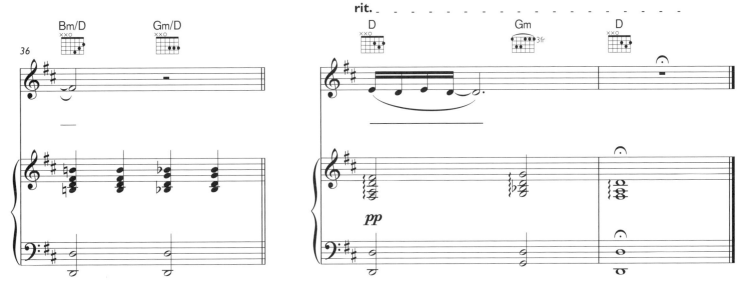

Misha Fox on trombone and Jermaine Amissah on baritone saxophone –
played on 'Tonight Tonight', 'Love Is Back' and 'Tell Me Something I Don't Know'.

Tonight Tonight

Words and Music by Celeste Waite, Jamie Hartman and Sean Douglas
© 2020 Warner Chappell Music Ltd administered by Eastman Pond Publishing, Warner Tamerlane Publishing Co and Reservoir 416
Warner Chappell Music Ltd, Warner Chappell North America Ltd and Reservoir Reverb Music Ltd

To-night, to-night, you're the place I go__ to, to-night, to-night, the

face I tell it all__ to, to-night, to-night, I just wan-na hold__ you

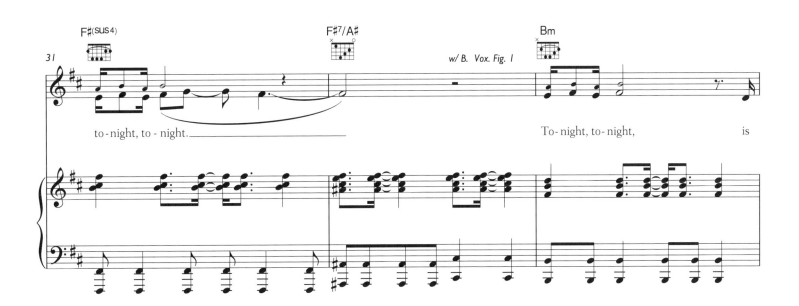

to-night, to-night._____ To-night, to-night, is

it too late to show you? To-night, to-night, my-self is who I owe you,

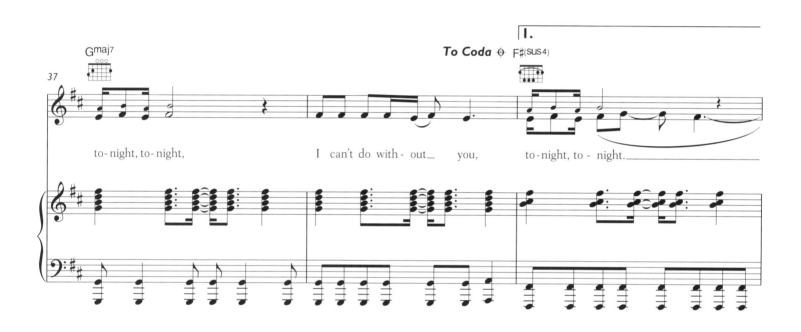

to-night, to-night, I can't do with-out___ you, to-night, to-night.___

2. I___ to-night, to-night.___ How can I hold

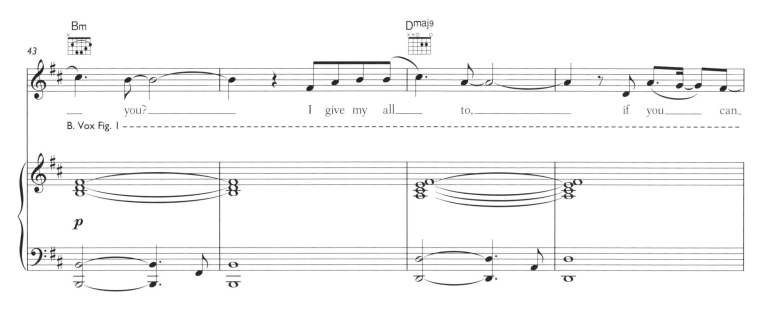

Left to right: Misha Fox on trombone, Jermaine Amissah on baritone saxophone and Kaidi Akinnibi on tenor saxophone.

Stop This Flame

♩ = 120

Original key: B♭ minor (one semitone higher)

pp

without Pedal

p

simile

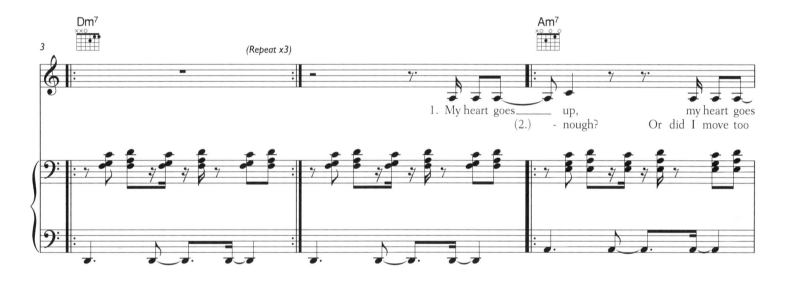

(Repeat x3)

1. My heart goes_____ up,   my heart goes
(2.) - nough?   Or did I move too

___ down,   we fall in___ love   and we fall back out. I'll give_ you
___ far?   Is it all too___ much?___   I think I must be mad___ to give you

To Coda

My good friend Jamien Nagadhana – bass player on
'Ideal Woman' and 'Tell Me Something I Don't Know'.

Jamie Haughton – we all let out a scream of excitement when he played that fill on 'Tell Me Something I Don't Know'. You can hear my yelp on the track.

Tell Me Something
I Don't Know

It could mean your silence with my heart the word
it's strong enough so I've heard
   You're mistaken me for your masterpiece
   Gilding me, so I try
frame me fallen take me as I came
   Or face the night alone
These Idle arms, I hold

I CAN BE BOLD
DECORATE ME
ADORE ME BABY
BUT I CAN'T BE OWNED
IT'S NOT PART OF MY DESIGN
I'LL LET YOU KNOW
WHEN I NEED YOU TO LIBERATE ME
I'LL HOLD MY POSE

Not Your Muse

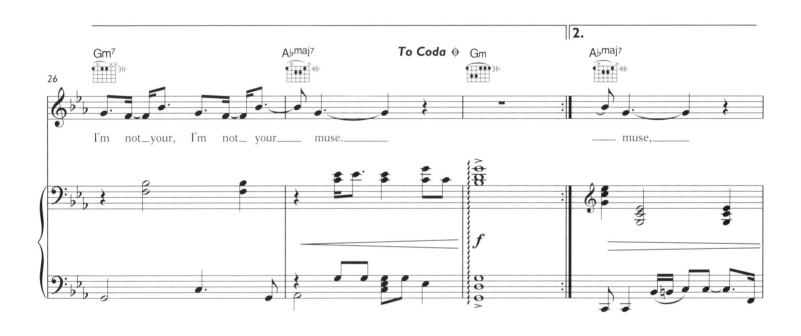

What have I got to do,— why give my - self to lose?—— You know me, dis-own me, come back to my start.——

D.% al Coda ⊕ **Coda**

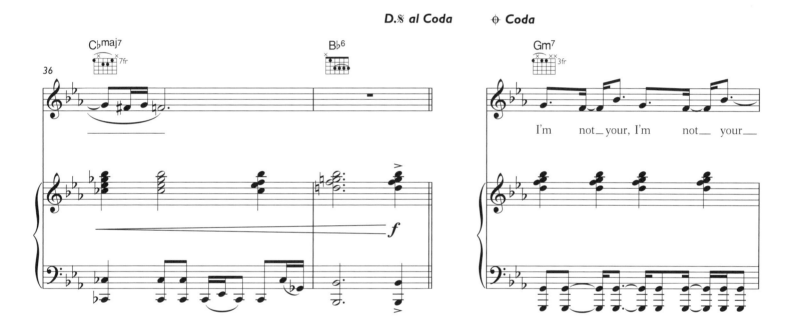

I'm not— your, I'm not— your——

— muse.—— I'm not— your, I'm not— your...——

BUT I'M NOT YOUR
   I'M NOT YOUR
   MUSE

I'M NOT YOUR MUSE

He came back to me
Like he knew he would
Didn't know the chance he took
Was one too far
Only I can steal the Good You've made
      of me
Anybody else could see
   It's in my palms
Get's easier to grieve
The morning sun
   to face the night alone
These idle arms that know

Beloved

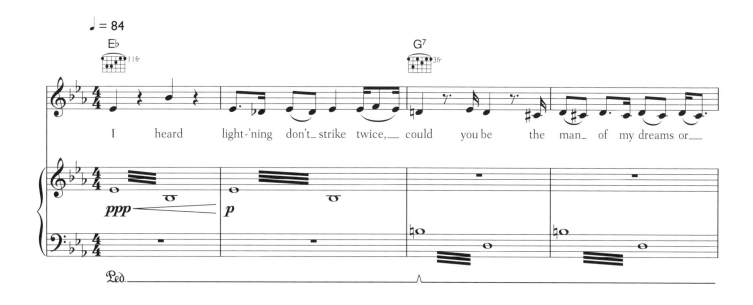

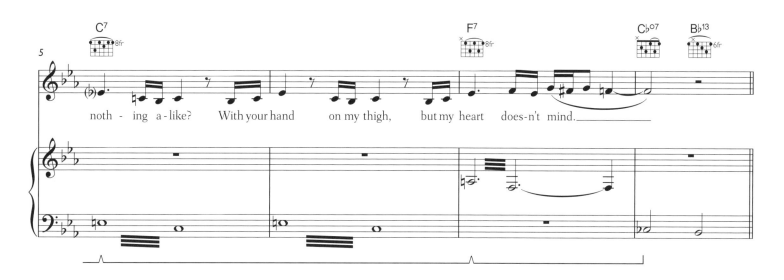

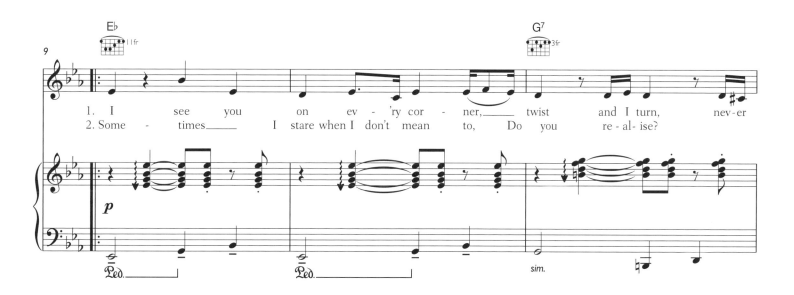

Kaidi Akinnibi – Saxophonist and arranger for the 'Love Is Back' horns section.

Love Is Back

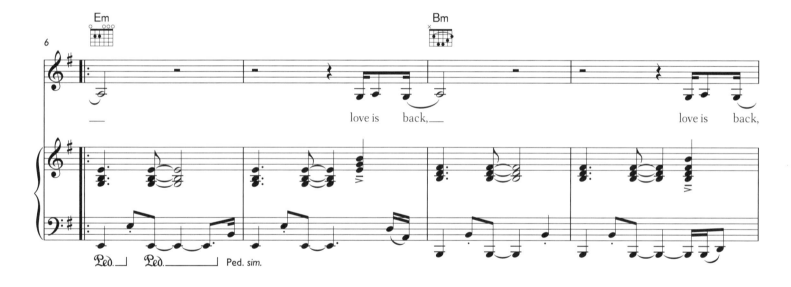

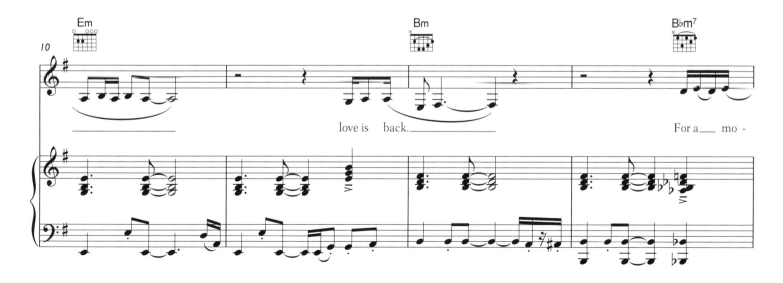

Words and Music by Celeste Waite, Jamie Hartman, Ettie Hartman, Kaidi Akinnibi, Dominic Canning, Jamie Houghton, Mark Mollison and Jamien Nagadhana

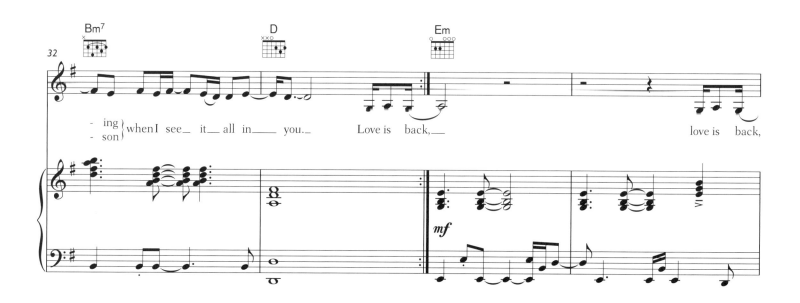

I hate to tell you but I,
could do no better and I
Would change the method if I could

It takes just one to lean in just one to
stop you speaking,

But words won't do you any good

A Kiss

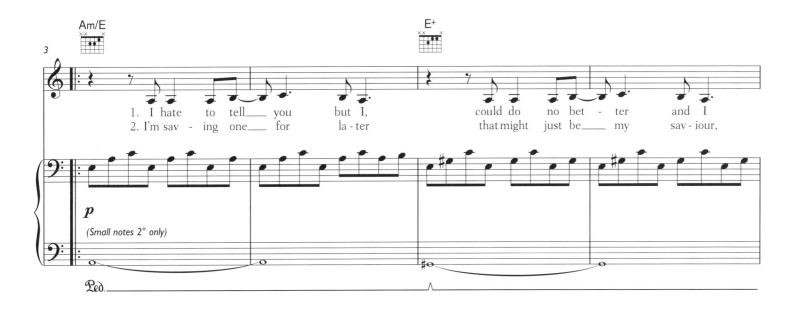

Words and Music by Celeste Waite, Robin Fredriksson, Mattias Larsson, Jamie Hartman and Mark Mollison

Walk away but tell me this human nature
as it is really doesn't mean
to be so Cruel

I'm saving one for later that might just be my
Saviour I'll only know then if I should.

THE PROMISE

Who is it, you again
Thought you left
But you never go to far
Remember when we overslept
That morning when
Our thing fell apart

But I never learn
I always and overtrust
I do it to myself
But I can't be burying
These feelings when
It's the best thing
I ever felt
since

You got my promise again
You had me pining when you left
Knowing it's been ages

I'm taking you in

But there's a little little urge ¡ me a

burn   tell

Maybe by September I
Would have tired enough
Of other stuff
To know that you weren't
right

But we never learn
We always lust
And over trust
It happens
Overnight

And I don't wanna be your
enemy
Or something you need to pass
the time
So excuse me if this comes off green
But, sometimes I just wanna go back
and rewind to those nights
                    everytime
But the problem is there's a part of me
and   urgency and
little burn that overturns your
the bird/ burden comes back
            to the everytime

The Promise

Words and Music by Celeste Waite, Kaidi Akinnibi, Jamie Houghton, Holly Millman, Mark Mollison and Jamien Nagadhana

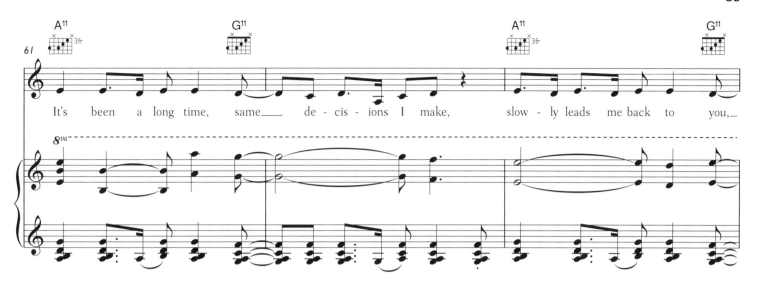

It's been a long time, same___ de - cis - ions I make, slow - ly leads me back to you,___

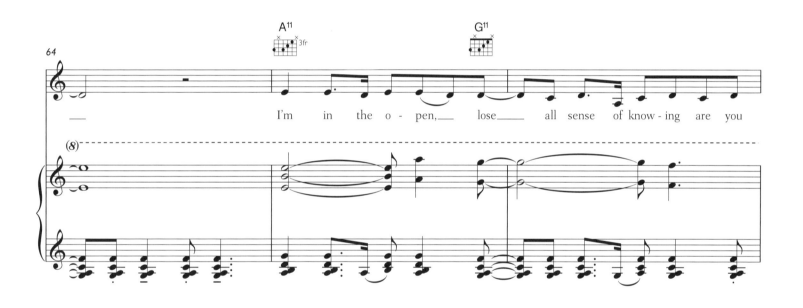

___ I'm in the o - pen,___ lose___ all sense of know - ing are you

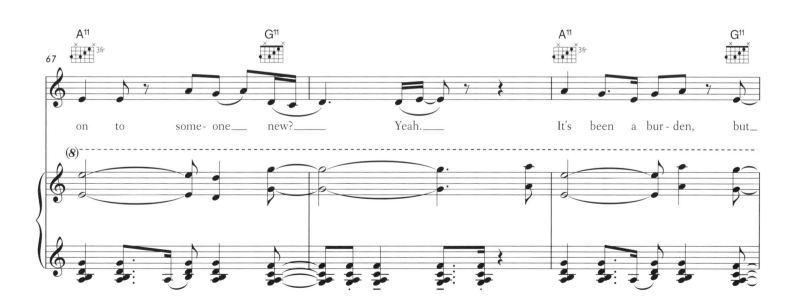

on to some - one___ new?___ Yeah.___ It's been a bur - den, but___

Happiness   home to nest
come back soon / be back soon
then I'll forget
the doom + gloom
if I give this ~~xxx~~ gift bit to you
will everybody feel/get a little love

Every gets a little love

Wouldn't
Would everybody get a little love

Give a little love and
    watch it move a mountain

Put it in your pocket
Watch it ~~xxx~~ a move a

~~Too good~~

~~Put it~~
    ~~you can't do without~~

~~Too good~~

watch it move a mountain
its now   found

Share it now you found it

A Little Love

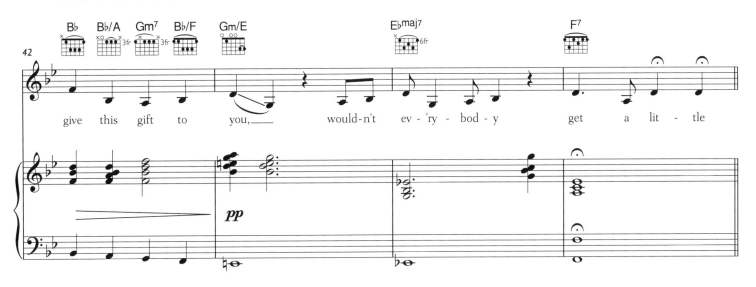

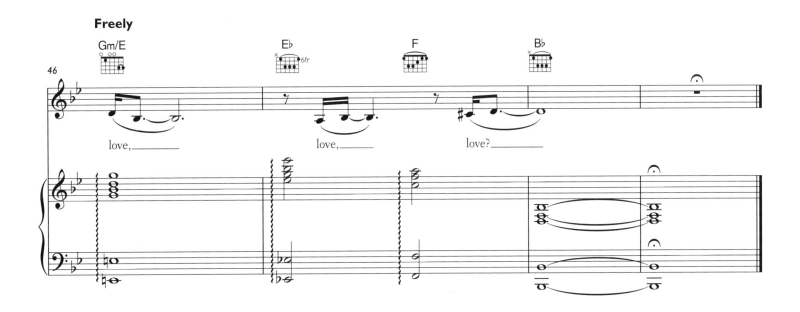

On a hot summer's day working out our parts for the song 'Not Your Muse'.

Some Goodbyes Come With Hellos

Words and Music by Celeste Waite, Jamie Hartman, Gregory Hein and Samuel Roman

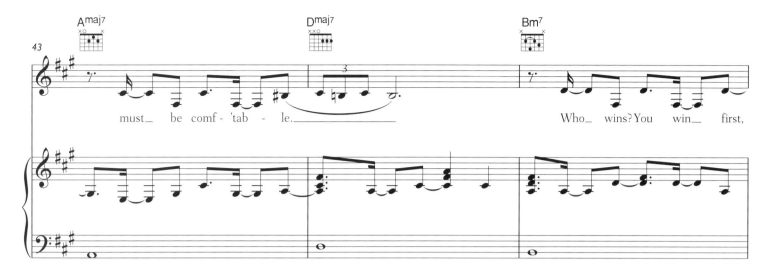

must_ be comf - 'tab - le._____

Who_ wins? You win_ first,

D.S. al Coda

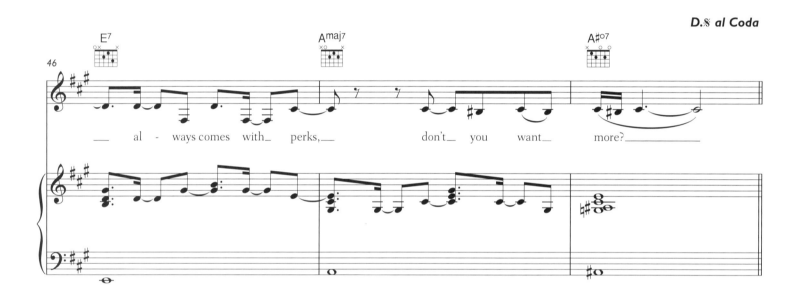

___ al - ways comes with_ perks,_

don't_ you want_ more?_____

Coda

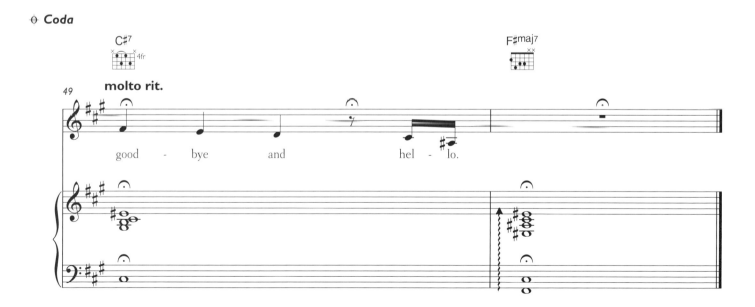

molto rit.

good - bye and hel - lo.

Having a quiet moment listening to a song that didn't make the album with producer Charlie Hugall.

Cover illustration by Celeste
Cover designed by Dominic Brookman
Music arranged by Olly Weeks
Edited by Lucy Holliday

© 2021 by Faber Music Ltd
First published by Faber Music Ltd in 2021
Bloomsbury House
74-77 Great Russell Street
London WC1B 3DA

Printed in England by Caligraving Ltd
All rights reserved

ISBN: 0-571-54207-7
EAN: 978-0-571-54207-9

To buy Faber Music publications or to find out about
the full range of titles available, please contact your
local music retailer or Faber Music sales enquiries:

Faber Music Limited,
Burnt Mill,
Elizabeth Way,
Harlow
CM20 2HX
Tel: +44 (0)1279 82 89 82

fabermusic.com